Praise for this book...

"This book is a compilation of correspondence from prison inmates to their dear friend and mentor in living for Christ in the spiritual darkness of their lonely prison cells.

I have known and worked alongside with the author, Virgalee Brooks, for nearly fifty years. I have come to appreciate her love for her Lord Jesus Christ. She has proven herself to be faithful, compassionate, and trustworthy in all matters of life and mission.

Virgie, as I know her, has shared her life and witness in a number of California state prisons and county jails and juvenile institutions. She has helped many men, women, and young people discover true purpose in their lives in relationship to God.

The precious letters in this book will give you a bird's eye view of the response that many prison inmates continue to express their love and appreciation for Virgie's life and mission. You will be challenged and blessed as you take time to consider each letter."

-Glenn L. Morrison
Founder and CEO
Follow Up Ministries International

"Hebrews 13:2 states that many of us entertain angels unaware. Over the years, Virgalee Brooks has tirelessly given herself, her time, and treasure to visit, encourage, and minister to those incarcerated. To these souls that others have given up on she must have been seen as an angel! What an inspiration and example of being salt and light in such a dark world. Now we celebrate in person the letters, poems, and exchanges from prisoners to Virgalee. Enjoy and be encouraged! We love you, Virgalee."

-Singles Pastor, Michael Cook
Calvary Christian Center
Sacramento, California

"Let you light so shine that men see your good works and glorify your Father which is in heaven. Virgie is that person that makes serving God look easy. The way she taught me gave me the desire to keep the Gospel simple. Sometimes teachers with big words and flowery quotes confuse the meaning. Virgie keeps it sharp and to the point in such a way you will always get the point. Virgie's two-edged sword has helped me be one of God's soldiers. I hope that the women of Chariots of Fire and I were good students. We love you, Virgie."

-Kimberly Harrison
Director of Chariots of Fire Women's Home
San Jose, California

"Virgalee Brooks has been the epitome of Isaiah 61:1. Bring the good news, binding up the broken hearted, and proclaiming liberty to the captives. She has touched many lives as she faithfully serves in prison ministry where so many are bound. We are blessed to have such a humble and willing servant, who shares her life's experiences as a testimony of God's faithfulness to all people. His promise not to break a bruised reed is evident in Virgalee's life. She gives those who feel trapped hope for a life of freedom. The poems and letters in this book are just a glimpse of the many lives Virgalee has touched."

-Anita M.
Captive: 1969-1993
Set Free: 1994

Letters From Prison

He has sent me to proclaim freedom for the prisoners

Virgalee Brooks

XULON PRESS

Foreword

One way to find out about a person is to read what others say about them. In this book, "Letters from Prison," you are able to read what others are saying about a lady I think is pretty special. You see, I too, at one time was one of the prisoners she visited. May these letters motivate, inspire, challenge, and encourage you to live a life that others will one day write about the impact you have had on them for the cause of Christ. Virgalee definitely fulfills the scripture that says, "I was in prison and you visited me."

-Dr. Samuel M. Huddleston
Assistant District Superintendent for the Assemblies of God
Northern California/Nevada

Table of Contents

Acknowledgments

My thankfulness and appreciation first go to my Heavenly Father, who has been and always will be my mentor, my teacher, my instructor, my guide, my counselor, my deliverer, my healer, and my comforter. It is because of His great love for me and the imparting of His wisdom, revelation, and spiritual understanding to me that I am alive today.

Next I want to thank my three beautiful children, Brian, Teresa and her husband Bill, and Stephen for their deep consistent love and encouragement. Also for my three precious grandchildren, Holly and Jennifer Wade, and Stephen M. Brooks. They have brought me so much joy, love, and laughter.

I will always be grateful and so appreciative of those friends who have consistently offered me their love, their expertise, their insight and persistent encouragement to not stop until this project was finished and they are: Sherry Grimes, Betty Jo and Pat Mullen, Reverend Glenn Morrison, Janie Snyder, Kelly Parsons, Reverend Pat Chapman, Kim H., Anita M., Dr. Phil and Brenda Goudeaux, Pastor Nehemiah Goudeaux, and Reverend Sam Huddleston.

A huge thank you to Dr. Mike Murdock, and Dr. Creflo and Taffi Dollar for their love and wisdom that they have poured into my life in great abundance.

I am forever grateful to my editor, Dr. Larry Keefauver, and the Xulon Press staff for their assistance in publishing this book.

Also to all the inmates whose love and commitment to keep in touch with me through their letters, poems, etc. is a joy and treasure beyond measure. I am sure my Heavenly Father will bless you all abundantly because of the blessing this book will be to many others.

Introduction

Love, Mercy, and Grace

This is a story that portrays the love, mercy, and grace of an almighty awesome God. A God who can take a life, heart, and mind that was totally shattered and broken in a million pieces, molding beauty out of ashes, giving the oil of joy for mourning, and putting on a garment of praise for the spirit of heaviness that He might be glorified.

God's love became very real to me as a thirteen-year-old girl lying in a hospital bed paralyzed with polio. I cried out to God with many tears asking Him to remove the paralysis from my legs. Four days later I walked out of the hospital without needing assistance from anybody, Praise God!

I became very hungry and thirsty for more of God and His Word, searching and reading the scriptures daily, wanting to know more of the wisdom, knowledge, and understanding of the Holy Spirit. I wanted more of His love and to know more about His love, mercy, and grace.

My Dad was a very abusive person filled with deep-rooted anger, rage, unforgiveness, and bitterness. His verbal, emotional, and mental abuse affected me deeply. There was frequent sexual molestation and sexual assault. All of this took place in a home where our parents took us to church three times a week. Dad spent several years in prison for his crimes. After he went to prison I also suffered sexual abuse and sexual assault at the hands of an older brother (now deceased).

When I had just turned eighteen years old, I was involved in a serious car accident. The doctors did not expect me to survive, but if I did there was a strong possibility that I would live in a vegetative state the rest of my life. I suffered a severe concussion, broken ribs, punctured lungs, cracked vertebras, internal injuries, etc. God performed another miracle by bringing about a quick healing which allowed me to return to my forty hour a week job within five weeks.

The most painful part of that experience was when my Dad said, "It would have been better if you had never come out of that car wreck alive."

My mother, sitting next to him agreed with him. The pain I felt emotionally and mentally was far more severe than my physical injuries. I did a lot of crying and praying, seeking the love and comfort of my Father God.

Several years later I married a man I thought was a good Christian man. We both sang in the choir and he taught Sunday School class. Later I discovered he was a paranoid schizophrenic with violent tendencies. There are no words that can adequately describe the hell that my children and I lived through. If my husband saw me reading the Bible or if he saw me praying, I would be beaten black and blue. He made several attempts to end my life, but God was very merciful to me and I am very sure God had guardian angels watching over us. My Heavenly Father helped us escape from that violent environment.

The road to recovery, healing, and restoration was very painful at times as we sought to recover from the wounds and pain that we had endured. I turned to the Word of God for instruction, wisdom, and guidance.

I learned some key elements to spiritual warfare through these scriptures

Psalm 32:8
Psalm 91
Psalm 34:19
Ephesians 6:10-18

God has given us the armor to defeat the devil, but we have to put it on and put it to use. I had to learn to take one step at a time, one day at a time because it was not going to happen overnight.

I also had to learn some key elements to achieve my emotional healing:

1. Choose to forgive.
2. Learn to walk in God's love and embrace it.
3. Keep a positive mindset. This one is a must!
4. Memorize and use the Four R's Principle:
   Rebuke
   Resist
   Reject
   Refuse

I had to apply these Four R's to anger, resentment, bitterness, unforgiveness, emotional hurt and pain, mental hurt and pain, revenge, spite, envy, etc.

Two scriptures that really helped me in this quest were Luke 10:19 and James 4:7. Using the four R's Principle has brought deliverance and healing to thousands of inmates who have found themselves behind prison walls in juvenile halls, county jails, and state prisons where I have had the privilege to go into for over thirty-three years as a God Squad'er.

I am a God Squad'er

What is a God Squad'er? It is a person who goes into prisons, jails, road camps, honor farms, work furlough centers, CYA, and Juvenile Hall. We also go into state and federal prisons.

What do we do when we get there? We sing, pray, conduct Bible study classes, and preach the Word of God. We laugh with the inmates, we cry with them, we encourage them, and let them know there is One who will never leave them nor forsake them. We tell them we love them and that we care what happens in their lives. We also do a lot of one on one counseling. They are hungry for love and acceptance and want to know the Word of God.

These inmates are full of questions like:

- *How do I make it once I get out?*
- *Can God help me stay out of prison or jail?*
- *Can He help me get a job once I get out?*
- *Can God help me get my kids back?*

They long to hear practical success stories, stories from people who have been down the same road or similar ones, and find out God has answers for every situation in His Word.

A lot of the juveniles are repeat offenders, but we must never stop trying to help them, love them and let them know you and God care what happens to them. Many of them are released from Juvenile Hall to go home to a Mom who is a junkie or a prostitute, whose father if there even is one is an alcoholic or heroin addict. They know what it is like to be beaten and sexually assaulted at a very young age.

I can tell them I know from my own experience what this is like and that there is only One who can heal a broken heart and crushed spirit. Jesus is the only One who can take away the pain, hurt, unforgiveness, and hatred that can destroy them. I tell them He did it for me and He will do it for them, too!

Most of them believe God is the one responsible for all the bad things that have happened to them. When they are shown in God's Word that it is the devil and not God that has been the culprit, they really light up and that look of hopelessness and despair goes away, and with it comes the revelation that God is truly a God of love. They get excited about what God is going to do in and through their lives.

Am I sorry about all the bad things that has happened to me? Not in the least, I am thankful and praise God every day for showing me His power, peace, and strength in the midst of the storm. After every storm there has been a rebuilding and a strengthening of what was once weak. I praise God for putting me in a jail or juvenile hall every week to help others and show them how He can help them, too. The most important thing I do is leave behind those who are drawn a little bit closer to Jesus because of the testimony of my life He has allowed me to share with them.

That is why I am a God Squad'er!

-Virgie Brooks

Winter, 2015

-1-

Living in Misery

I was living in deep misery
In heartbreak, grief and shame;
Behind the walls of prison
With a number for my name.

My friends they all forsook me,
My loved ones put me down.
But behind these cold, gray walls of stone
A new life I have found.

Now I live my life for Jesus!
And He means the world to me.
My body is behind these prison bars,
But my soul is alive and free.

I no longer have the urge to hate
But a strong desire to love
And every hour of each day
I pray to my God above.

The Devil Is a Liar

Sister Virgie,

First giving all honor to God, our Lord and Savior Jesus Christ. I just want to thank the Lord for saving my soul and not letting me die in sin.

I was a terrible person, I did not care about myself. I was on drugs doing whatever it took to get them. I was very mean and violent, on a very fast broad road to hell. When I was at my lowest, King Jesus stepped in and told me to stop holding to my dead mother, father, drugs, alcohol, and to hold on to life eternal, which I could only find in Jesus Christ, the Son of the living God—the only God. He showed me the devil was a liar and the father of all lies. Also that the Holy Spirit who lives in my body is the spirit that raised Jesus from the dead and who gives life to my mortal body.

I thank God for loving me and I do love Him. I am a conqueror just as the scripture says in Romans 8:28. So my beloved brothers and sisters, let us do as it says in Hebrews 13:5-6 and keep our lives free from the love of money and be content with what we have, because God has said, "Never will I leave you; never will I forsake you." So say with confidence, "The Lord is my helper, I will not be afraid. In the Word of God I have an anchor, my soul is anchored in the Lord!"

Your sister in Christ Jesus,
Bonnie

God's Love Letter to You

Are you living in misery today? You too can be set free from the lies of the devil. His whole purpose is to convince you that you have done so many bad things in your life that there is no hope for you. He will tell you no one can ever love you including God. Do not believe those lies! God has written a letter to you in His Word, the Bible. Here is His love letter to you today:

> *For God so loved the world the he gave His only Son,*
> *so that **everyone** who believes in him may not perish*
> *but may have eternal life.* (John 3:16 NRSV)

Do you see that word **everyone** in that letter to you? When God says everyone, He means everyone—that includes you. Now read the next part of this letter written especially for you:

> *Indeed, God did **not** send the Son into the world to*
> ***condemn** the world, but in order that the world might*
> *be **saved** through him.* (John 3:17 NRSV)

God does **not** want to condemn you, He wants to **save** you. Do you want to be saved from a life of misery? Do you want to know what to do to be saved by your God who loves you so much He sent His own son to pay the ransom to release you from the lies of the devil? The next part of God's love letter tells you what you need to do to obtain this salvation:

Those who believeth in him are not condemned.
(John 3:18)

If you confess with your lips that Jesus is Lord and believe in your heart that God raised him from the dead, you will be saved. (Romans 10:9 NRSV)

Time to implement the Four R's Principle:

Rebuke the lie of the devil.
Resist the temptation to believe God cannot love you.
Reject the feeling of condemnation, it is not from God.
Refuse to wait another minute, turn to God today!

Please accept this wonderful gift from the God who loves you. Tell God you believe Jesus died for your sins and all of your wrong doings. Tell Him you believe Jesus paid the price and that God raised Him from the dead so you can be set free from the lies of the devil. Ask Jesus to be your Lord and Savior today, right where you are. Thank God for giving you this wonderful gift of love!

Write to me and tell me all about it at vbrooks@volcano.net.

Look Up! Look Up!

Look up, look up your redemption draweth nigh
As long as you look up, you won't worry, you won't sigh.
Just keep your eyes on Him the one that's up above
For soon He'll be coming, He'll be coming for His beloved.

I've found that while in prison, my trials are not so sweet
But I keep looking up, for my King I'll soon meet.
I know that He is coming and I know that it won't be long
So tho' the trials get heavy, I'll keep praising in a song.

I know things look bad, that old dollar is fading away
Sometimes I know you wonder, if you'll make it another day
But my "sister" if you'll look up and keep your eyes on
that old cross
Then rejoice and don't worry, for your soul won't be lost.

Now as I close this song, for really I must go
I hope you are encouraged to run on to the shore.
Remember on this journey, when you don't feel too high
Just keep on looking up, for your redemption draweth nigh.

"God Bless You as You've Blessed Me!"

Yours in Christ, Sam

A Breath of Freshness to Our Souls

Hello Sister Brooks,

I'm so grateful to God for the blessing it has been knowing you. When I read your letter I just started praising God-thank you Jesus, for my sister Virgie. Halleluiah! You have really blessed my soul. Sister, it was your letter that inspired me to move on. Thank you. You see so many had doubted that I could learn, so I began to doubt-but, oh, your letter-God bless you.

All the brothers are rejoicing over your letter. Please don't stop writing to us, please. Your letters are a breath of freshness to our souls. God is really using you in a ministry of encouragement to others. You take care and from all of us, we love and thank God for giving us a sister named Virgie Brooks. Keep looking up, your redemption draweth nigh – Glory.

In His Name, Your brother, Sam

God's Love Letter to You

Jesus says to you today, *"The Father himself loveth you, because you have loved me and have believed that I came from God"* (John 16:27). *"We are God's children and we can call Him, Father"* God's Word tells you in Romans 8:15-16.

Where are you looking?

Are you looking at how bad things are for you?

Are you looking down on yourself and doubting yourself?

Do you know what God says about you?

You can say with Sam and others who have doubted whether or not they can change because it says in God's Word, "I can do all things through Him, [Jesus Christ] who strengthens me" (Philippians 4:13).

Look up because that is where your help comes from. God is the only one who can show you the way to becoming the person He knows you can be.

Time to implement the Four R's Principle:

Rebuke the lie that says you cannot learn.
Resist the temptation to doubt yourself.
Reject the fear of failure.
Refuse to give up.

Will you tell Father God that you want Him to help you become all that He wants you to be? Thank Him for all the love and help is giving you today. Believe in yourself because God believes in you and says you can do it!

-Write to me and tell me what you are doing about it at vbrooks@volcano.net.

-3-

I'm On the Winning Side

There is oh, so very much garbage in my life...
So full of sin and so full of strife.
You'd think I'd know this is not God's plan
So against the devil I shall take my stand.

No more of the devil's garbage will I take on my back
For that will just get me off the narrow track.
When Jesus shed His blood on that old rugged tree
It was for strength and power to have victory.

Victory over sin, victory over self and loneliness
And all those other things that bring so much stress.
It is God's plan for me to be on the winning side
For if I follow Him my feet will never slip nor slide.

Virgalee Brooks
December 27, 1985

The Race Is On

For over twenty-five years I was a silver medal runner for Satan. Whatever you can think of, I did it. Searching to achieve, but always falling short of my own expectations.

The love of my family has always been mine to hold, but I was still constantly searching for something, someone to fill the emptiness within. My teen and adult life passed by quickly-too quickly and the searching went on. Without hope of finding any peace or love to fill the emptiness in my heart. Have you ever been in a crowd and still felt alone? If so you can relate to how I felt.

After two husbands and two daughters I turned to heroin and cocaine thinking it to be the answer. Knowing to well it could and would destroy me, but the loneliness inside made it easy to believe the lies whispered to me in my ear. At no one's hands but my own, heroin and cocaine became my wake-up, night-cap and everything in between.

The Lord called on me several times throughout my life. The enemy never makes it easy for us to go to the Lord for refuge, unless we know how. Although we are ALL offered the gift of salvation. AMEN! On November 5, 1989 on my knees with repentance in my heart the Lord forgave me and rescued me from myself. With His arms opened to me I went with a tear streaked face and surrendered my heart to Him. All at once the emptiness was filled with joy and peace. I was no longer alone. While thanking Him, I could hear Him telling my heart "Fear not, for I am with you. No longer will you be alone. Call unto me, I will never leave you." THANK YOU JESUS!

On February 18, 1990 I buried the old me forever in baptism. Although the race is still not over I know I can and will be victorious.

PRAISE GOD! I strive to be a gold medal runner for the Lord Jesus Christ. When I needed a word of encouragement He laid this on my heart, "I can do all things through CHRIST which strengthened me" (Philippians 4:13).

Join me in the race for the Lord. Our reward awaits us in Heaven. On your mark, get SAVED and let's go to heaven where He waits for us all with His arms opened wide. I want the gold, how about YOU!

A runner for Jesus,

Annie

Convict for the Cross

Dear Virgie,

Just a few lines to introduce myself and wish you blessings over the holidays. The Lord is my light and might. As for myself while in prison a lot has happened. One morning about 5: A.M., while everyone was asleep, tired from yelling and laughing to keep from crying, I laid awake alone with just my memories, Jesus knocked at the door of my heart and I answered it. He took away all jealousy, greed, pride, and starving for sex I had in me. He became my country and I his soldier.

Before I met Jesus I was just a carefree child, running wild. To win I cheated but instead I lost, but now Jesus is here to help me pay the cost. In the future I plan in what I hope will be, Jesus taking me to heaven to be eternally free. I can write an endless book on how I feel toward my Savior, but nothing can express the feeling of magic I felt inside of myself when I read my favorite scripture for the first time 1 Corinthians 13:4-7 out of the Living Bible.

May God love you, shower His blessings upon you. Once I was lost but now I'm found in the love of Jesus Christ.

Love,

Gary

Love is very patient and kind, never jealous or envious, never boastful or proud, never haughty or selfish or rude. Love does not demand its own way. It is not irritable or touchy. It does not hold grudges and will hardly even notice when others do it wrong. It is never glad about injustice, but rejoices whenever truth wins out. If you love someone, you will be loyal to him no matter what the cost. You will always believe in him, always expect the best of him, and always stand your ground in defending him. (1 Corinthians 13:4-7 TLB)

God's Love Letter to You

Many inmates believe that God is the one responsible for all the bad things that have happened to them. When they are shown, in God's Word, that it is really the devil who has deceived them (and not God), they really light up with a look of hope. Despair goes away with the revelation that God is truly a God of love. They get excited about what God is going to do in their lives and through their lives. It is amazing to see the changes in them when they realize they are now on the winning side.

Here are some of the scriptures I give these new "gold medal runners for Christ."

1 Corinthians 9:24-27 says, "In a race everyone runs, but only one person gets first prize. So run your race to win. To win the contest you must deny yourselves many things that would keep you from doing your best. An athlete goes to all this trouble just to win a blue ribbon or a silver cup, but we do it for a heavenly reward that never disappears. So I run straight to the goal with purpose in every step. I fight to win. I'm not just shadow-boxing or playing around. Like an athlete I punish my body, treating it roughly, training it to do what it should, not what it wants to. Otherwise I fear that after enlisting others for the race, I myself might be declared unfit and ordered to stand aside" (TLB).

What does this passage tell you about being a "gold medal runner for Christ"?
Are you running the race with purpose?
Are you fighting to stay on the winning side?

Hebrews 12:1-3 says, "Since we have such a huge crowd of men of faith watching us from the grandstands, let us strip off anything that slows us down or holds us back, and especially those sins that wrap themselves so tightly around our feet and trip us up; and let us run with patience the particular race that God has set before us. Keep your eyes on Jesus, our leader and instructor. He was willing to die a shameful death on the cross because of the joy he knew would be his afterwards; and now he sits in the place of honor by the throne of God. If you want to keep from becoming fainthearted and weary, think about his patience as sinful men did such terrible things to him" (TLB).

> *What is holding you back from running the race God has placed before you?*

> *Are you keeping your eyes on Jesus as your leader and instructor?*

Time to implement the Four R's Principle:

Rebuke the devil for trying to put all that garbage on your back.

Resist the temptation to take your eyes off of Jesus.

Reject the stress the devil is trying to place on you.

Refuse to allow your circumstances to prevent you from running your race.

> *Can you say with these "gold medal runners for Christ" I can do all things through CHRIST which strengthened me (Philippians 4:13)?*

-Write to me and tell me how this helped you get back on the winning side and running your own race at vbrooks@volcano.net.

-4-

Someone Cares

Someone cares and always will
The world forgets but God loves you still
You cannot go beyond His love
No matter what you are guilty of
For God forgives until the end
He is your faithful, loyal friend
And although you try to hide your face
There is no shelter any place
That can escape His watchful eye
For on the earth and in the sky
He's ever present and always there
To take you in His tender care
And bind the wounds and mend the breaks
When all the world around forsakes
Someone cares and loves you still
And God is that someone who always will.

Sally wrote the following three months after an attempted suicide:

Discovering daily who God really is
Thanking him daily, he's mine and I'm his
Discovering daily God's great love for me
Such mercy, forgiveness, amazingly free
Discovering daily that God really cares
Discovering daily he does answer prayers
Discovering daily what grace really means
Unmerited favor beyond all my dreams
Discovering, discovering each day that I live
That all I need, he freely will give
Discovering daily Christ working through me
Accomplishing daily what never could be
Discovering daily that I can't, but he can
Thanking him daily for the place in his plan
Discovering daily how real life can be
When I'm living in Christ, and he's living in me
Discovering daily a song in my heart
With anticipation each day to start
Delighting and basking in love so divine
Secure in the knowledge I'm his and he's mine
Besides contentment, excitement I see
A daily adventure, Christ alive and living in me.

God's Love Letter to You

One night in Juvenile Hall I found myself talking to a very angry and frustrated teenage boy. I encouraged him to read some key verses in the Word of God (the Bible) and then to talk to God for himself. He did not know how to start so I gave him a couple of instructions on how to start communicating with God. When I went back the next week I found a very excited young man. He handed me, "A Note From Heaven" and said this is what God spoke to him. He was thrilled that he could talk to God and that God really wanted to talk to him.

A Note From Heaven

I see your loneliness and fears, your guilt and frustrations. I see your endless search for love and fulfillment. All this must be in order for you to come to the end of your own understanding, then you can hear my voice. Listen carefully amid the noise of the world and you will hear...

I love you, I shed my blood for you to make you clean. Give yourself completely to me. I created you to be just as you are, and you are lovely in my eyes. Do not criticize yourself or become depressed for not being perfect in your own eyes. This only leads to frustration, I want you to trust me one step, one day, one second at a time. Dwell in my power and my love and be free, be yourself. Don't allow other people to control you. I will guide you, if you will let me, but be aware of my presence in everything.

I give you patience, love, joy, and peace. Look to me for answers for I am your shepherd and will lead you. Follow me only and do not ever forget this. Listen and I will tell you my will.

Let my love flow from you and spill over to all you touch. Be not concerned for yourself...you are my responsibility. I will change you without your knowing it. You are to love yourself and love others, simply because I love you. Take your eyes off yourself, look only at me. I lead, I change, I create, but not when you are striving. You are mine...

Let me have the joy of making you like Christ. Your only command is to look to me and me only, never to yourself and never to others. Do not struggle, but relax in my love. I know what is best, and I will do it in you. Stop trying to become, and let me make you what I want. My will is perfect, my love is sufficient. I will supply all your needs...only look to me. I love you!

Your Heavenly Father,

AMEN

Andy

December 26, 1985

Juvenile Hall Inmate

As you read this note from heaven, what parts really touched your heart?

What was the only command God is giving you through this note?

What promises did God make to you in this note?

Read these additional verses that will reinforce these promises from God to you. Write out your own note from heaven as God communicates with you through His Word.

John 10:1-16 which says _____ is the Good Shepherd and is willing to _____

_____.

Psalm 23 reminds us the Lord is our shepherd and will

_____.

Time to implement the Four R's Principle:

Rebuke the noise of the world around you.

Resist the temptation to criticize yourself.

Reject what the world says about you and only believe what God says is truth.

Refuse to become depressed or frustrated knowing God is in control.

-Write to me and tell me how knowing Jesus is your shepherd has changed your life at vbrooks@volcano.net.

With Jesus

With Jesus, Oh yes, with Jesus
There is a peace in every storm
And with His love to surround us,
We're safely sheltered in His arms.

With Jesus, Oh yes, with Jesus
Those steep mountains we'll surely climb
No matter how rocky it may seem
We'll reach the top in His good time.

With Jesus, Oh yes, with Jesus
Those fiery trials won't seem so long
For when they're over then we will know
That when we're weak He is so strong.

With Jesus, Oh yes, with Jesus
We'll have no more than we can bear
He will give us the strength to stand on
And with the world His love to share.

Virgalee Brooks
February 18, 1976

But Now, I Have Jesus

I can still hear the words, "but now I have Jesus, but now I have Jesus." The minister spoke them last night.

Jesus, you started them ringing over and over, louder and louder within my heart until everything else was drowned out—all except my own painful sobbing.

Tonight again with tears streaming down my face. I feel my woman's heart beating faster in a love response. Last night I had felt like a woman desolate and forsaken, struggling alone for fulfillment and desperately seeking after your love, but Jesus, you never had left me, and again I hear the echo of, "but now I have Jesus."

Once again, Jesus, you are proving your love to me. I am not a rejected woman but chosen and loved, oh so tenderly by you. I know, Lord, you will not let me go! Tonight, as you are drawing me closer I feel your hands gently wiping my tears because "now I have Jesus."

Oh, such greater consolation in knowing that You have me for keeps! You drew me away from the crowd only because you so desired to draw me closer to Yourself. I was unfaithful as I hoped that another man could satisfy my lonely despairing heart.

Please keep teaching me, beloved Lord, to desire Your love more than a man's love. Love me in the way I so passionately crave to be loved. Only you, Lord, know how to love me this way.

Dear Virgie,

As this letter reaches you, I hope that it finds you basking in the bosom of God's love. The Lord Jesus Christ is so merciful and so loving. I just praise Him in everything I do. I never thought I would love the Lord as I do right now today. I can't begin to tell you how

He's watched over me and how He continues to keep His hand on me always. I can't tell you how much our Sunday Bible Studies help me make it through the week here, and also how the Lord continues to pave the way for me. I ask Him every day to wash me with the blood of Jesus.

Virgie, your testimony was wonderful! I would have never thought that you'd have gone through so many trials. Boy, I tell you there's nothing, I mean nothing in the world like the love of the Lord Jesus. I want to thank my Heavenly Father for the joys, peace, and the sorrows because without those sorrows I would never have known the glory of your love. I just want to magnify your Holy Name.

Satan and his workers are working hard against me. My husband wrote to tell me he wanted to separate and he feels that would be better. I prayed and told my Lord that if it is His will for this marriage to be finished, then I accept it, but if not, in the name of Jesus I rebuke the lies of Satan. Well, about a week later my husband wrote me and said he was going through something, he didn't want to end this marriage, and we are going to make it. So I guess I got an answer from above, right?

Love,
Cherie

God's Love Letter to You

For I'm going to do a brand-new thing. See, I have already begun! Don't you see it? I will make a road through the wilderness of the world for my people to go home, and create rivers for them in the desert! (Isaiah 43:19 TLB)

Read these verses that ministered to me that night that I wrote, **But Now, I Have Jesus.** Record how God ministers His love to you through each one of these love letters to you.

Romans 8:28 promises: _____

Psalm 73:28 says God will be my_____

Psalm 46:10 tells me to _____

Isaiah 41:10 promises: _____

Time to implement the Four R's Principle:

Rebuke the lies of Satan that say your marriage or your family or your life is over.

Resist fear and face your challenges knowing God has got your back.

Reject what Satan is trying to use to disrupt your world.

Refuse to accept defeat because God will give you the victory.

-Write to me and tell me how this chapter has encouraged you to stand up and fight for your marriage, your family, and your new life in Christ at vbrooks@volcano.net.

-6-

Jesus Is Always Near

Realities
The Things I Saw

While sitting here in this prison cell
Everything looked as gloomy as hell.
I thought I'll write a poem to say just what I feel,
Because what I'm about to say, "It's Real."

I started thinking about the past
And the many days that I did waste
Living my life at a fast crazy pace
But really never "winning" the ultimate race.

I glance out my tiny window and strain my eyes to see
I look into the sky and there my life stood before me
I saw the past and the present and there was shock on my face
Things looked so senseless with nothing to trace.

The rays of the sun seemed to make a few things clear
And there I saw the face of Jesus so very near
I rubbed my eyes and thought it all an illusion
And then I saw my life's conclusion.

I saw some things that only I know
The old words came to my mind, "you reap what you sow."
I looked into the sky and asked God to bend down His ears
The prayer I said brought a shower of tears.

I confessed I was a sinner and asked Him to forgive my sins
He said only through His beloved son Jesus were my sins forgiven
So I bowed my head and this is what I said....

"Jesus, I know you died for all my sins and transgressions
So here's from my heart-an honest and true confession.
I asked Him again, this time with a little meaning in my voice.
He said, "I thought you'd never come back to me, it's always been
your choice."

And from that moment on things seem crystal clear
Because I now know "Jesus" will always be near.

Darlene
Aug. 14, 1990
N.C.W.F.

Worry Is Not of God

Dear Virgie,

I thank God for the opportunity to fellowship with you and to be
a dear friend of yours and most of all, you are my real sister in the
Lord (smile). I hope we can do something together in the future.

I have five months left to do here. I'm making goals and things aren't working out the way I would like. I know that I just have to hold on and wait on the Lord. He is the only one that can make something out of nothing. The Holy Spirit is dealing with my spirit. All good things come to those who wait. All things are working together for the good of them who love the Lord and are called according to His purpose, and I know I am called/chosen by God to be a light to shine in the midst of darkness (smile).

It's been so long since I have walked down the streets and seen cats, dogs or traffic. I know the Lord will be walking with me. Keep me in prayer for peace to live the last few months here just one day at a time and not to panic about what I am going to do about this or that.

I have so much to be thankful for and the little that I have will become much when I place it in the Master's hand. I know God won't leave me hanging, He is faithful for that's what His Word promises. God has not stopped working on me yet. Seems like He makes me learn everything the hard way.

I wish I could spend more time in your class. I will be there the next couple of weeks because our Bible College class will be out for a while. I admire your faithfulness to God and the ministry and the kind of person I would not mind working with.

God loves you and so do I.

Your sister in Christ,

Sara

God's Love Letter to You

"So my counsel is: Don't worry about things—food, drink, and clothes. For you already have life and a body—and they are far more

important than what to eat and wear. Look at the birds! They don't worry about what to eat—they don't need to sow or reap or store up food—for your heavenly Father feeds them. And you are far more valuable to him than they are. Will all your worries add a single moment to your life?

And why worry about your clothes? Look at the field lilies! They don't worry about theirs. Yet King Solomon in all his glory was not clothed as beautifully as they. And if God cares so wonderfully for flowers that are here today and gone tomorrow, won't he more surely care for you, O men of little faith?

So don't worry at all about having enough food and clothing. Why be like the heathen? For they take pride in all these things and are deeply concerned about them. But your heavenly Father already knows perfectly well that you need them, and he will give them to you if you give him first place in your life and live as he wants you to. So don't be anxious about tomorrow. God will take care of your tomorrow too. Live one day at a time." Love, Jesus (Matthew 6:25-34 TLB)

Circle the words that reflect worry in your life:

Concern	Apprehension	Anxiety	Fear	Burden
Uneasiness	Disquiet	Lack of Peace	Disorder	Discomfort
Lack of Joy	Pain	Depression	Anxiousness	Distraught
Sleeplessness	Agitation	Nervousness	Dread	Distress

What do you need to do to get rid of these symptoms of worry in your life?

Time to implement the Four R's Principle:

Rebuke those thoughts that try to bring worry into your mind and heart.

Resist the urge to worry about things that are beyond your control.

Reject anything or anyone that tries to make you worry when you know God's in it.

Refuse to allow worry to paralyze you and keep you from being what God has called you to be.

-Write to me and tell me how you are overcoming worry in your life at vbrooks@volcano.net.

-7-

"She Reached Out To God Today"

She reached out to God today.
He reached back and took her hand.
Then she pled, between her sobs,
Please help me if you can!

He gave her hand a gentle squeeze,
So his presence, would be known.
And said, "My precious, precious child,
Now you'll never be alone."

She began to look real frightened,
So she closed her eyes real tight.
Was this all just a dream?
Or was God, really here tonight?

He spoke again, real softly,
As he wiped away her tear.
"There is no need to cry, my child,
As long, as I am near."

"And there is no need to worry.
There is no need for fear.
If you ever need me,
You know I am always near."

"So don't be afraid, little one.
Don't run away and hide.
I said you'd never be alone,
I'd be right at your side."

"And if you still doubt my love,
Look back and you will see;
I was there and squeezed your hand,
Whenever you really needed me."

She replied:
"Oh God, I wish I'd heard you say,
'My child I'll always care.'
If I had, when things got bad,
I would have known
You were always there!"
Sandy

Give Jesus Your Burdens

Dear Sis,

Praise the precious Name of Jesus. Hallelujah! I love Matthew 11:28-30. God is so good! Ever since I've come back in February He's healed my broken heart, and cured my sick soul. My body which I had mistreated with pills, alcohol, and dope the Lord has restored. Healing is God's will for me.

I have often been mixed up, frightened, and sick. Now I give to God my soul, my body, and my mind. There is completeness in Christ. I rejoice in the health of my total being, blessed be God who heals me.

God is doing such a work in our hearts here at Sierra. Boy! Are we ever fortunate, you know we have peace in abundance here compared to other joints. I'm receiving a hundred fold return myself (Mark 10: 29-30), and you can believe me I'm T-H-A-N-K-F-U-L! My Heavenly Father cares for me! Praise God!

Your friend and brother,

Jerry

God's Power Touched My Heart

Dear Virgie,

You have truly broke that bondage, Satan had a hold of my emotions. Two days before your seminar Satan was on full attack. I have been saved by God's grace and mercy since Feb. 11, 1998. Through God's mighty power I feel you were talking directly to me. You are full of the mighty power of the Holy Ghost. You have made me feel alive, so very alive. Your seminar has made me so strong and so much hungrier for God's Word. Through His grace and mercy you touched on a lot of things I was struggling with, your encouragement is so strong. I felt everything you were saying through your teachings and your testimony. God's power has truly put a strong touch within my heart, it can never be erased, it is so pure and whole. You have mightily helped me make a complete turn around. Thank God!

I love you,

Your sister, Rhonda

God's Love Letter to You

"Come to me and I will give you rest—all of you who work so hard beneath a heavy yoke. Wear my yoke—for it fits perfectly—and let me teach you; for I am gentle and humble, and you shall find rest for your souls; for I give you only light burdens." Love, Jesus (Matthew 11:28-30)

We all serve something or someone. God has given us freedom to choose whom we will serve. A great leader in the Bible challenged his people with these words, "But if serving the LORD seems undesirable to you, then choose for yourselves this day whom you will serve, whether the gods your ancestors served beyond the Euphrates, or the gods of the Amorites, in whose land you are living. But as for me and my household, we will serve the LORD" (Joshua 24:15 NIV).

What are you choosing to serve?
What have been your rewards?
Do you need to change whom you will serve?

Those who choose to serve the Lord receive a truly amazing reward. Read these verses and discover for yourself the benefits of serving God instead of those things that bring destruction into your life. Describe each benefit.

Matthew 16:26-28 _____

Matthew 6:33 _____

Colossians 3:23-24 _____

Proverbs 13:21 _____

Psalm 1:1-6 _____

Time to implement the Four R's Principle:

1. *Rebuke those people or things that seek to place you in bondage.*
2. *Resist anyone or anything that seeks control over you.*
3. *Reject thoughts that impede your progress and take them captive instead.*
4. *Refuse to allow anyone or anything to place you in bondage ever again.*

-Write to me and tell me how Jesus has set you free from those things that had been keeping you in bondage at vbrooks@ volcano.net.

-8-

Tell It to Jesus

When your heart is full of trouble and there are
teardrops of despair
Do not cry and pine and worry—tell it to the Lord in prayer.
Pray to Him for love and comfort when your
troubles make you cry—
He is always in your presence with the comforts life denies.
Tell Him of the grief and heartaches that are burdens in your life
And wishes that you pray for to calm your tears and strife.
He will touch your heart with comfort and with
His love of Holy Grace
In a sanctity of Blessings and the warmth of His embrace.

Blessed be God who did not refuse me the kindness I sought in
prayer (Psalm 66:20),
Betty

I Am Not Ashamed of the Gospel

Dear Sister Virgie,

As usual, I am a little slow in answering your letter. I really enjoyed the service last Thursday night, in fact, I enjoyed it much more than I thought I would. Bro. Juan did indeed preach a good message. I am looking forward to seeing you and all the brothers and sisters that come up with you.

I feel great and the power of the Lord has been working steadily for me. As Paul said, "I am not ashamed of the Gospel, it is the power of God for salvation to everyone who has faith" (Romans 1:16). I feel that faith more and more every day. It has changed my thoughts, my actions, and my whole way of life. Nothing is more powerful, I have never felt as free and pure as I do now, even with being in prison. The prison my heart and mind was in was much worse. I am free, free in the Lord and I will remain that way because I know I have faith in Jesus Christ and His Father.

Things are working out so well for me. God's grace and love are performing wonders in my life. When I begin to relate my life today with that of my past, I wonder why I waited so long to accept Jesus and His teachings to guide my life and decisions that I make.

My mother and I have been completely apart for the past seven years. A short while ago I decided to try and change that. So I wrote her, explaining my change of attitude and relationship with God and His son, Jesus. She answered and for the first time in eight years we will be visiting on June 30.

It is great to know I will once again see my mother. God is so good to a sinner like me. God Bless you and your family, pray for me.

Love, Your brother in Christ,

Joe

God's Love Letter to You

The only letter I need is you yourselves! By looking at the good change in your hearts, everyone can see that we have done a good work among you. They can see that you are a letter from Christ, written by us. It is not a letter written with pen and ink, but by the Spirit of the living God; not one carved on stone, but in human hearts. We dare to say these good things about ourselves only because of our great trust in God through Christ, that he will help us to be true to what we say, and not because we think we can do anything of lasting value by ourselves. Our only power and success comes from God. He is the one who has helped us tell others about his new agreement to save them. We do not tell them that they must obey every law of God or die; but we tell them there is life for them from the Holy Spirit. (2 Corinthians 3:2-6 TLB)

We are all God's love letter to those who have not yet discovered His great love for them. We are to show God's love to even the unlovable through our acts of love as God's ambassadors.

So from now on we regard no one from a worldly point of view. Though we once regarded Christ in this way, we do so no longer. Therefore, if anyone is in Christ, the new creation has come: The old has gone, the new is here! All this is from God, who reconciled us to himself through Christ and gave us the ministry of reconciliation: that God was reconciling the world to himself in Christ, not counting people's sins against them. And he has committed to us the message of reconciliation. We are therefore Christ's ambassadors, as though God were making his appeal through us. We implore you on Christ's behalf: Be reconciled to God. (2 Corinthians 5:16-20 NIV)

God Squad Team Members help those who are incarcerated to discover God's truth, we leave behind lives who are drawn a little bit closer to Jesus because Jesus is there with us, working through us! We seek to make an eternal difference in the lives of those Jesus loves! You can be a God Squad Team Member in your work place, neighborhood, and community.

What can you do to begin to act as Christ's ambassador in your workplace?
In your neighborhood? In your community?
What does Matthew 5:16 challenge you to do today?

Time to implement the Four R's Principle:

1. *Rebuke the idea that you are only one person and cannot make a difference.*
2. *Resist the temptation to let others act as Christ ambassadors in your area.*
3. *Reject those old mindsets and reach out in love to others God sends you to.*
4. *Refuse to become complacent. God is calling you to be His ambassador.*

-Write to me and tell me how you are stepping out as Christ's ambassador in your workplace, neighborhood, and community at vbrooks@volcano.net.

-9-

Hurt—To Heal

I cried, "Lord, use me!"
He answered, "Wait."
Then came the hurt.
Loneliness—I walked through desolation to share His fellowship.
Doubt—I wept through despair to seek His faith.
Fear—I wrestled through darkness to seize His freedom.

And the Balm of Gilead flowed into the depths of my soul.
It cleansed. It soothed. It healed.
Again I cried, "Lord, use me!"
This time He answered, "Go!"
"I send you forth to heal."
"Walk with the lonely—share with them my fellowship.
Weep with the despairing—seek with them my faith.
Wrestle with the fearful—seize with them my freedom.
And the Balm of Gilead will flow into the depths of their souls.
It will cleanse. It will soothe. It will heal."
He spoke again: "My child, I spared you no hurt
That I might use you to heal!"

You Are Like a Mother to Me

Dear Mama Virgie,

Grace and peace be to you from God, the father of our Savior Jesus Christ. I attended the seminar here at Cook County Jail. I just wanted to let you know from my heart you are appreciated. I also want to thank each of you for allowing the spirit of truth to move you with such compassion to share with us.

It seems like I have known you for a long time. You are like a mother to me. I just pray that you will continue to share the message of salvation, and to inform each of them that Jesus loves them. He assures us that we have hope, love, joy, and peace once we accept Jesus into our lives. He takes away all that pain, sorrow, and guilt. He removes all shame and burdens you may carry around. He teaches us to give Him all our burdens and anxieties and He will deal with them.

Thanks to people like you whom Jesus uses to get the good news across that He loves and has a purpose for us all in life (Jeremiah 29:11). God has seen fit to use me to lead many others to know Him.

Also He has entrusted me with the task of Staff Clerk for a counselor here. I don't get paid for this job here, but I feel responsible. I haven't worked since I was fifteen years old, I am thirty now. The big picture I see is He is entrusting me with these talents as it is written in Matthew 25:14-30 and once I prove to be faithful here, He's going to open greater tasks for me out there. Now I do know that He is not going to put on me more than I can bear (1 Corinthians 10:13). So as long as I keep the words He's given me in the meekness of His wisdom I'll be alright (James 3:13).

I truly miss you all and I definitely love you all, so keep in touch.
I am going to close now with love for you all and keep you all in my
prayers. May God continue to bless you all in everything you do.
Love you, Mama Virgie,
Johnny

God's Love Letter to You

"For I know the plans I have for you," declares the Lord, "Plans
to prosper you and not to harm you, plans to give you hope and a
future. Then you will call upon me and come and pray to me, and
I will listen to you. You will seek me and find me when you seek me
with all your heart. I will be found by you, and will bring you back
from captivity." (Jeremiah 29:11 NIV)

God's Word is full of so many promises to you. Read these
verses and bask in His love for you. Write these verses out in your
own words and record why they are so meaningful to you. Be pre-
pared like Johnny to share your talents with others.

Matthew 25:14-30
1 Corinthians 10:13
James 3:13

Time to implement the Four R's Principle:

1. *Rebuke the idea that God cannot use you to help others.*
2. *Resist the temptation to let the pain and hurt paralyze you.*
3. *Reject the burdens of the past, give them to Jesus.*

4. *Refuse to live in fear, use the talents God has given you for good.*

-**Write to me and tell me how you are using the talents God has given you to help others vbrooks@volcano.net.**

-10-

Broken Things

My Saviour specializes
In mending broken things;
He takes the heart that's shattered
And gives it songs to sing.
He pieces it together
With His sweet gracious touch;
He mends the heart that's broken
Because He loves so much.

He mends the broken spirit,
Then lifts that spirit up…
And pours the oil of gladness
Into the upturned cup.
The broken lives He reshapes…
Those lives so wrecked by sin
When in their crushed condition
They turn in faith to Him.

The broken dreams that crumble
To ashes at our feet
They seem so fair and lovely
That made life taste so sweet…
Those broken dreams He rebuilds

And fashions them anew…
Then gives us faith to trust Him
To see new dreams come true.

Thank You for Your Letters and Prayers

Dear Virgie,

Thank you for the card and most of all for your prayers. It is real comforting to know someone out there cares for us in here. There are trials that you go through in these places, but it is hard on our families. There is no way we can keep our families together. Only God can do this for us. But thank God for people like you who care enough to come and help us by ministering to our hearts and by praying for us and our families. I am thankful for God's mercy for us. I speak for myself when I say we are undeserving of God's mercy, but I ask for it for my family and myself. I long to know His will in my life and in my family's lives.

Thank you for your prayers and concern for us here and our families. God bless and prosper you and your family,

In Christ,

John

Dear Virgie,

I just wanted to take a moment to thank you for your kindness and devotion to share your time here. This place is surrounded by so much negativity and it is such a blessing when you come and do Bible Study with us. I truly appreciate all that you do. The ink pens, reading materials, and all that you give in addition to your time. I have been blessed I still have faith and hope. I am fighting this negative atmosphere all the way.

I miss my children and family so much. I now have a release date. So pretty quick now I will be home. I still haven't made any definite decisions yet. I am planning on rebuilding my life one step at a time. My family has been very supportive through this though. I believe our paths will cross again one day outside of these walls.

Love,

Darlene

Dear Virgie,

I received your letter this week and I was so happy to hear from you. I have missed you for two whole Sundays. I really look forward to studying under your teachings from Jesus. I know you have been praying for me because I feel the power of your prayers. Things continue to happen that are blessings from above. I am trying to be obedient and do God's will—often it is very heard, but I love Him, so I keep trying!

Well, Virgie, I hope to see you soon and we all love you. Stay strong in Jesus.

Love you,

Joanie

Dear Virgie,

Thank you so much for your letter. It really makes me feel good to know that people care. I used to have a hard time understanding why people would care about me. I use to think they must want something in return. But now, when I have nothing to give, I see there are people like you showing that you care and that I matter.

Thank you,

Carla

God's Love Letter to You

Five times I received from the Jews the forty lashes minus one. Three times I was beaten with rods, once I was pelted with stones, three times I was shipwrecked, I spent a night and a day in the open sea, I have been constantly on the move. I have been in danger from rivers, in danger from bandits, in danger from my fellow Jews, in danger from Gentiles; in danger in the city, in danger in the country, in danger at sea; and in danger from false believers. I have labored and toiled and have often gone without sleep; I have known hunger and thirst and have often gone without food; I have been cold and naked…. I was given a thorn in my flesh, a messenger of Satan, to torment me. Three times I pleaded with the Lord to take it away from me. But he said to me, "My grace is sufficient for you, for my power is made perfect in weakness." Therefore I will boast all the more gladly about my weaknesses, so that Christ's power may rest on me. That is why, for Christ's sake, I delight in weaknesses, in insults, in hardships, in persecutions, in difficulties. For when I am weak, then I am strong. Sign, Apostle Paul (2 Corinthians 11:24-27 and 12:7-10 NIV)

Time to implement the Four R's Principle:

1. *Rebuke the idea you are too broken to be fixed.*
2. *Resist the negativity that tries to overcome your faith and hope.*
3. *Reject your crushed condition and turn in faith to Him.*
4. *Refuse to give up hope.*

-Write to me and tell me how God is using you to help others mend their broken lives and dreams vbrooks@volcano.net.

-11-

God Uses the Imperfect to Accomplish His Perfect Plan

God can use you.

Remember…

Noah was a drunk.

Abraham was too old.

Joseph was abused.

Gideon was afraid.

Samson was a womanizer.

Rahab was a prostitute.

David was a murderer.

Jonah ran from God.

Peter denied Christ.

The disciples fell asleep while praying.

The Samaritan woman was divorced several times.

Zaccheus was too small.

Paul was too religious.

Lazarus was dead!

God can use you, too, just as you are,

To your fullest potential,

In the circle of His love.

Prayers from Prison

"Right now Lord we come before You in agreement because it says when two or more gather in Your name, there You are in the midst. Please help me in my mind, I get so weak and feel I am falling, Lift us up Lord, so we can proclaim Your promises and works wherever we are. Teach us Your ways, enabling us to be a reflection of You always." -Paul

God Is Faithful

While reading Isaiah 40-45 I took cheer in our Lord's longsuffering towards us, His forgetful people. His tender mercies, warm compassion, and loving care are continually bestowed upon us, as undeserving as we are. He promises to restore us when we fail, to that joyful gentle fellowship of life Himself. Many times I have endured pain and suffering. I even wanted to break fellowship with such a wonderful God, yet He beckoned to me through friends, wooed me with His indwelling Spirit, and brought to remembrance His Word. But still I set my face toward the glamor of the world. His permissiveness allowed me to go and have my fill of sinful desires.

Being apart from God had a very disastrous effect on my life and attitude. As my inhibitions dwindled, my little white lies grew, I went from occasional drinking to drunkenness, craziness, stealing, and carousing in sexual sin that almost killed me. All these finer things of the world are what my flesh demanded until I finally repented and tossed my hope to the wind. But He loved me enough that when my pleasures had wreaked havoc in my life, He guided me back to Him with His perfect love, and began to displace the ugliness that sin had

63

caused. The precious love I forsook. I've found that anything I displace Christ with is a counterfeit, regardless of the outward attractiveness or innocence. Living for the flesh leads to separation from God, ruin, and death.

I've found in Jesus a quality of life I never lived before. It's richer, fuller, and more rewarding as I take the time to cultivate my relationship with God. I've become more dependent upon Him for daily victory, which He is providing through the teaching by His blessed indwelling Spirit. I'll be released from total incarceration to total freedom soon. I hope to continue a biblically structured program outside. I believe our Father will use me in giving instruction and guidance to victorious living, which are in Christ alone, to my Christian ex-convict brothers. –D-

Taking It to the Streets

Last weekend we had a seminar here with four ex-cons who have gone on from here to various forms of ministry. It was excellent and very informative to the men who have some doubts about taking their Christianity with them to the streets. All of these men were here serving time at one point or another and have made a very real change in their lives. -Joe

God's Love Letter to You

For the message of the cross is foolishness to those who are perishing, but to us who are being saved it is the power of God. For it is written: "I will destroy the wisdom of the wise; the intelligence of the intelligent I will frustrate." Where is the wise person? Where is the teacher of the law? Where is the philosopher of this age? Has not God made foolish the wisdom of the world? For since in the wisdom of God the world through its wisdom did not know him, God was pleased through the foolishness of what was preached to save those who believe. Jews demand signs and Greeks look for wisdom, but we preach Christ crucified: a stumbling block to Jews and foolishness to Gentiles, but to those whom God has called, both Jews and Greeks, Christ the power of God and the wisdom of God. For the foolishness of God is wiser than human wisdom, and the weakness of God is stronger than human strength. Brothers and sisters, think of what you were when you were called. Not many of you were wise by human standards; not many were influential; not many were of noble birth. But God chose the foolish things of the world to shame the wise; God chose the weak things of the world to shame the strong. God chose the lowly things of this world and the despised things— and the things that are not—to nullify the things that are, so that no one may boast before him. It is because of him that you are in Christ Jesus, who has become for us wisdom from God—that is, our righteousness, holiness and redemption. Therefore, as it is written: "Let the one who boasts boast in the Lord." (1 Corinthians 1:18-31 NIV)

You, an everyday person, can be something special and significant in an enormous, hurting world. You can be love right where you are. Christ makes all the difference. Allow Him to mend your brokenness and then share His love with everyone you meet!

Jesus said to His disciples, "The harvest truly is plentiful, but the laborers are few. Therefore, pray the Lord of the harvest send out laborers into His harvest" (Matthew 9:37-38).

You can do this because:

> You are chosen by the will of God and saved by the grace of God;
>
> You are held by the love of God and empowered by the Spirit of God;
>
> You are guided by the Word of God and protected by the hand of God!
>
> That's why God can use you to implement His perfect plan!

Time to implement the Four R's Principle:

1. *Rebuke those who say God cannot use you.*
2. *Resist the lie that you are too bad to be God's messenger.*
3. *Reject the mindset that you need to be perfect before God can use you for His glory.*
4. *Refuse to allow anyone to keep you from doing your Father's work.*

-Write to me and tell me how God is using you to carry out His perfect plan at vbrooks@volcano.net.

-12-

Facing Our Mountains

Praise to the Lord, glory to the highest.
God accepted me, so He can't be biased!
Jesus loves me and Jesus loves you.
So whatever the problem is, He will see you through.
The Lord is my Shepherd, He's all I need.
When sin clouds my life, my case He will plead.
Since we've done it on our own, and life has been tough,
Call on Jesus Christ for He's more than enough!
-Darrell

When faced with a mountain, God can give you creative and unexpected solutions to your obstacles!

You Made My life More Bearable

Dear Virgie,

That was real nice of you folks to share with us in the way that you did. To this day I remember and will always remain grateful to God for people as loving and caring as you folks. Thanks to all the good people who along with you made my life more bearable under the circumstances.

Love,

Jerry

Learning to Trust the Lord

Dear Virgie,

I've got to do my Father's business, because He's sure taken care of mine. He's truly kept me, Sister. Renewed my mind, given me a new heart, and a strong desire to serve Him in spirit and in truth. You were a great part of my spiritual growth. You've taught me a lot, especially about being faithful to the Lord. Praise God for His keeping and restoration power.

Love,

Nancy

Dearest Virgie,

Thank you very much for your letter. I especially like the part about learning our prayers. It was my first time learning a prayer and I thank God for the will to learn it. My next project is Psalm 91. I know that will bring a smile to your face!

Once again, thank you for your constant ministering at Santa Rita Jail every Sunday. I must tell you, Virgie, I've desired the Lord to work for me on a certain problem that I promised I would let Him handle. But every day in the back of my mind I think about it. I trust the Lord, I believe in His presence, His power, and His love. Please pray for me to relax and let the Lord do His work. I realize I can make it. I will continue to learn as much as I can from you and through His Word. My heart is lighter now and your letter showed me that my true friends are those in the Lord—and you are my first. Thank you for your concern. I'll see you Sunday.

Love,

Joan

Dear Virgie,

Today is my first day in this prison. It is going to be a challenge to maintain my walk with God, but Jesus will see me through. Tonight I throw all my sins overboard and start walking with the Lord, my only true friend.

Love,

Stan

God's Love Letter to You

Jesus told them. "For if you had faith even as small as a tiny mustard seed, you could say to this mountain, 'Move!' and it would go far away. Nothing would be impossible. (Matthew 17:20 TLB)

For this is the love of God, that we keep His commandments. And His commandments are not burdensome. For whatever is born of God overcomes the world. And this is the victory that has over-come the world—our faith. Who is he who overcomes the world, but he who believes that Jesus is the Son of God? (1 John 5:3-5 NKJV)

You are an overcomer. You have the authority to speak to any mountain, any obstacle, and any circumstance that will keep you from fulfilling what God has called you to do. Picture yourself facing that mountain with Jesus standing right behind you carrying you on His shoulders and backing up your faith with His power and love.

Read Romans 8:31-39.

Describe what this passage means to you in your own life especially in regard to the "mountains" you are currently facing.

Time to implement the Four R's Principle:

1. *Rebuke that mountain.*
2. *Resist the temptation to turn away from that mountain.*
3. *Reject defeat.*
4. *Refuse to give up until that mountain has been conquered.*

-Write to me and tell me how God has helped you face and conquer your mountain at vbrooks@volcano.net.

-13-

The Armor of God

Heavenly Father,

We desire to be obedient by being strong in the power of Your might. We put on the armor that You have provided, with gratitude, praise, and by faith for spiritual protection against the forces of darkness.

Jesus is Truth. We confidently take the belt of truth, as strength and protection. We ask for wisdom and discernment to believe, live, speak, and know on the truth.

Thank you for the breastplate of righteousness. By faith we appropriate the righteousness of Jesus Christ and ask You to walk in Your holiness in our lives today.

Thank You, Lord, for the shoes of peace. We stand on the sold rock of peace as we walk in obedience to You, knowing You promise to walk with us.

Eagerly, Lord, we lift up the shield of faith. By faith, we trust in You to be our complete and perfect shield.

Our minds are a target for Satan's deceiving ways. Therefore, we take the helmet of salvation, knowing the Lord Jesus Christ is our salvation. We shield our heads with Him and invite His mind to be in us.

With joy, we take hold of the sword of the Spirit, the Bible, affirming that it is the infallible Word of God. Enable us to use Your Word to defend us from Satan and to claim Your promises.

Thank You, Lord, for the gift of prayer. We know this keeps our armor well oiled. Grant us a burden for others and enable us to see their needs and assist them through prayer as the enemy attacks them. (Ephesians 6:10-11)

Put on the Armor of Light

Dear Virgie,

Well, praise the Lord! Thank you for the short note of love. Also I receive the beautiful cassette tape last week and have listened to it many times. The Lord is so good to His children. I praise His name for having a beautiful sister like you! Rejoice! Rejoice in the Lord always!

Tell your family and friends that I say Hi and send my love. Tell your pastor I will be glad when I can give him a hug and praise the Lord with him. Also tell the brothers and sisters that came to Jamestown to rejoice in the Lord always for He is so good and does all things well—remember all things work together for good.

In His Love,

> *Mark— "The night is far spent, the day is at hand. Therefore let us cast off the works of darkness, and let us put on the armor of light"* (Romans 13:12 NKJV).

Full of the Holy Spirit

Dear Virgie,

I want to let you know that I miss you. You are in my prayers. I'm praying that you will come back soon. Me and the other girls need you. I thank God for you, you have so much strength. It's like it poured out of you into my heart. I thank God that you an awesome woman of God.

Virgie, the last day of your class when it was over I was so full of the Holy Spirit, I came running out of the class with my spirit rejoicing, I felt so strong. You are a shining light to the world. I thank God He has put you on my path. I love you and please pray for me. I have been smoking for sixteen years. I gave my tobacco away and asked my mother not to send me anymore cigarettes. I want to completely stop.

I am doing the Bible Study on the Book of Genesis. I feel my mind is in bondage—the devil does not want me to finish. But he's not going to stop me. He has no power for greater is He that is in me than is in the world.

God bless you.

Your sister,

Janet

God's Love Letter to You

The Lord will fight for you; you need only to be still (Exodus 14:14 NIV). *The Lord your God, who is going before you, will fight for you* (Deuteronomy 1:30 NIV). *Our God will fight for us* (Nehemiah 4:20). *The weapons we fight with are not the weapons of the world.*

On the contrary, they have divine power to demolish strongholds (2 Corinthians 10:4).

Wearing your armor well means walking in the fullness of the spiritual protection each piece gives you. God has not left you defenseless against the devil. He has equipped you with all you need to not only survive but to overcome any attack the enemy sends your way.

Isaiah 54:17 says no weapon formed against you will_____

_____.

What does that mean to you personally?

What battle are you facing right now in your life?

Are you wearing your armor?

Time to implement the Four R's Principle:

1. *Rebuke the attack of the enemy.*
2. *Resist his advances.*
3. *Reject fear and take your stand knowing you will be victorious.*
4. *Refuse to allow the enemy to gain a foothold in your life again.*

-Write to me and tell me how you are using the armor of God to stand against the enemy and with your battles at vbrooks@ volcano.net.

-14-

Life's Rainbow

One day I'll find my rainbow, but it will be a different kind.
Instead of finding a pot of gold, I'll find peace of mind.
I'll look at bright new mornings, a sky that's oh so blue.
I'll gaze at golden sunsets as every day is through.
I'll walk through lovely meadows, their beauty I'll behold.
I'll look for all the wonders of life that are untold.
I'll seek out all my neighbors who may need a helping hand.
I'll tell them if they have faith, their world will look just grand.
I'll always be most thankful to our Father up above,
For showing me life's rainbow that He filled with all His love.

You Made My Day Brighter

Dear Virgie,

I got your card yesterday. It was good to hear from you. Just knowing that people outside care makes my day a lot brighter. Thank you so much for thinking of me.

I gave a few of the girls your poem. They all liked it, I am going to send a couple of them to my family. It was a very special poem and I enjoyed it very much.

I am going to see my daughter Sunday. I am looking forward to it very much. I sure do miss her. Being away from her has sure made me realize what mistakes I have made. But I do think it's done me a lot of good. I might have ended up dead if I would have stayed out on the streets. That's where I was headed when I came in here. I looked half dead anyway.

Hoping to hear from you soon. Take care. Thank you for everything you have done for me.

Love,

Linda

The Real Me Is Coming Out

Dear Sister Virgie,

Thank you so much for your most welcomed letter. I've had some changes to go through. It seems like this old vase is getting an overhaul, but praise the Lord because I know that His guiding hand is upon me. There is so much self to die to, but it is beautiful because it is the real me coming out. The plain old me sees so much beauty in this world, feels so much at times too much yet there is still another side of me that is yearning to be released that it hurts.

It is always a blessing when you all come up. It is such a beautiful testimony to the Lord. There aren't many groups that come up to Sierra Conservation Center, I mean all kinds of worldly do, so the big question here among the men is, "Why the only entertainment they get is Christian?" Well, I just enjoy telling them that it is a voluntary situation, that the reason Christians do it is out of love and they don't expect or want any sort of pay. The worldly groups want money, so it is a beautiful witness.

I'm looking forward to seeing you all the next time you come up. May the love of our Father enhance your life and those you come in contact with.

Love in Christ,

Robert

God's Love Letter to You

His divine power has given us everything we need for a godly life through our knowledge of him who called us by his own glory and goodness. Through these he has given us his very great and precious promises, so that through them you may participate in the divine nature, having escaped the corruption in the world caused by evil desires. (2 Peter 1:3-4 NIV)

What evil desires are you battling in your life?

What corruption is the world trying to pull you toward?

What promises of God have you read about in this book that will help you stand against these negative influences in your life?

Time to implement the Four R's Principle:

Rebuke the corruption of the world.

Resist evil desires.

Reject anything that is contrary to God.

Refuse to associate with anyone or anything that pulls you away from God.

-Write to me and tell me how God's precious promises are changing your life for the better at vbrooks@volcano.net.

-15-

A Thanksgiving Prayer

Oh, God,
When I have food help me to remember the hungry;
When I have work, help me to remember the jobless;
When I have a warm home, help me to remember the homeless;
When I am without pain, help me to remember those who suffer;
And remembering, help me to destroy my complacency and bestir
my compassion.
Make me concerned enough to help, by word and deed,
Those who cry out for what we take for granted.
Samuel Pugh

Jesus tells us: "I am for you; I love you; I believe in you; I will be
with you; I will bless you; I will provide for you; I will strengthen
you; I will give you rest; I will answer you." – R. L.

Counting God's Way

A new day soon will begin, praise God, for He made it for you.
You are the child of His secret acclaim.
The world as it spins is inscribed with your name.
Time was devised for your wayfaring,

The trumpets of morning will be declaring.
This is your moment, only believe it.
Whatever your heart's hope, you can achieve it.
This is truly a Holy Day, as God has made it.
We should rejoice, for God has allowed us to live in it!

Always count your gardens by the flowers,
never by the leaves that fall.
Count your days by golden hours, don't remember the clouds at all.
Count your nights by the stars, not by the shadows or fears.
Count your life with smiles, not by your tears.
But most of all, with joy of every day, count your age by friends,
not years!
-Roy

God's Love Is Beautiful

Dear Sister Virgie,

The Lord has been very good to me, His love is beautiful and feels so good. Sister, I am glad you love the Lord the way you do. There's no greater joy than to love Jesus, for He is true love. I guess that's what the whole world is looking for, but we always try everything else first. I continue to thank God for your ministry.

Last year did not end well for me. Still I am excited about my growing relationship with Jesus. He is our light in the midst of our dark circumstances.

They really have a good fellowship at this prison. Our congregation is still going strong. We have some men who are serious about seeking the face of God. I still teach a few times a month. A few weeks back I taught a lesson on hope. God is good. Teaching God's Word is a real source of peace for me. I like to see the men's faces light up when they finally can make scriptural sense of something they are going through. I am singing in the choir, that's out of my comfort zone, but I want just want to serve the Lord.

Love,

Billy

In Service to God

Dear Virgie,

This is just a note from us to you to tell you how much we love and appreciate you. Thank you for caring and thank you for sharing your life with us. We so appreciate the example you show us by the life you live. Thank you for your courage as you live. You will probably never know how many lives you have touched or to what extent. When you are in the service of your fellow man, you are in the service of your God.

Love,

The Girls at Santa Rita Jail

God's Love Letter to You

But God is so rich in mercy; he loved us so much that even though we were spiritually dead and doomed by our sins, he gave us back our lives again when he raised Christ from the dead—only by his undeserved favor have we ever been saved—and lifted us up from the grave into glory along with Christ, where we sit with him in the heavenly realms—all because of what Christ Jesus did. And now God can always point to us as examples of how very, very rich his kindness is, as shown in all he has done for us through Jesus Christ. Because of his kindness, you have been saved through trusting Christ. And even trusting is not of yourselves; it too is a gift from God. Salvation is not a reward for the good we have done, so none of us can take any credit for it. It is God himself who has made us what we are and given us new lives from Christ Jesus; and long ages ago he planned that we should spend these lives in helping others. (Ephesians 2:4-10 TLB)

Write your own love letter to God. I would love to read it. Send it to me at vbrooks@volcano.net.

Conclusion

Thanks God Squad

I'd like to say thanks to all you folks
From the fellas dressed in blue.
You've helped us all so very much
We could never repay you.

You've helped us keep that blessed hope
That frees a man from sin,
By directing us through God's Holy Word
That's able to make a man win.

You've prayed with us so many times
Asking God to see us through.
So now we want to say thanks
To each and every one of you.

You've come to visit in the fog.
You've come in rain or sunshine.
Not once did you ever seek a fee,
You've never asked for a dime.

You've always come with a smiling face,
You don't know what that did for me.
And when you'd leave I'd always say
I'm in prison but yet I'm free.

Oh, thank you God Squad so very much
For your ministry to us in prison.
Because you are so faithful to Christ
His Spirit in us has risen.

So as we begun, we close the same,
Thanks from all of us to you.
Because you took the time to share with us
Heaven will be filled with guys in blue!

Sam Huddleston
January 14, 1978